The Cotswolds
in old picture postcards

by
Charles Hilton

European Library - Zaltbommel/Netherlands MCMLXXXVI

GB   ISBN 90 288 3345 5 / CIP

© 1986 European Library - Zaltbommel/Netherlands

European Library in Zaltbommel/Netherlands publishes among other things the following series:

IN OLD PICTURE POSTCARDS *is a series of books which sets out to show what a particular place looked like and what life was like in Victorian and Edwardian times. A book about virtually every town in the United Kingdom is to be published in this series. By the end of this year about 175 different volumes will have appeared. 1,250 books have already been published devoted to the Netherlands with the title* **In oude ansichten.** *In Germany, Austria and Switzerland 500, 60 and 15 books have been published as* **In alten Ansichten;** *in France by the name* **En cartes postales anciennes** *and in Belgium as* **En cartes postales anciennes** *and/or* **In oude prentkaarten** *150 respectively 400 volumes have been published.*

For further particulars about published or forthcoming books, apply to your bookseller or direct to the publisher.

This edition has been printed and bound by Grafisch Bedrijf De Steigerpoort in Zaltbommel/Netherlands.

INTRODUCTION

The Cotswold Hills, composed of oolitic limestone, are in Gloucestershire, with some fringing into Oxfordshire and Worcestershire. The area is unique, and the reason lies in the fact that its geological and historical continuity is almost perfect. There is a harmonious interrelationship between buildings and their natural environment. The stone weathers to a silver-grey, but also exhibits a sandy-buff colour with orange and purple variations. For centuries, churches, houses, buildings, and walls have been built of it, so imparting both beauty and character to the countryside, and an air of timelessness.

In the Cotswolds, everything is mixed up, but there is a uniformity of architectural style which, over the centuries, has depended upon skilled craftsmen applying similar methods in building. Hence, Tudor, Georgian and Regency houses are at harmony one with another. Today, in many Cotswold villages, building in stone is obligatory in order to conserve this harmony.

The Cotswold Hills vary in height between 300 feet to just under 1,100 feet at Cleeve Hill above Cheltenham. The high wolds of 800 feet or so are exposed to gales and rain, but the wide wolds of the north, east and centre consist of highly developed arable fields and improved pastures to suit modern mechanised farming. Sheep and dairy farming today have decreased with the advent of intensive cereal-growing. The gullied slopes of the west are well-wooded, and it is their streams which once powered the corn and cloth mills.

Man has populated the hills continuously since the New Stone Age. These early settlers have left their burial chambers known as long barrows. Later, the Celts buried their dead in round barrows. Many of the artefacts used by them are to be seen in museums in most Cotswold towns. For instance, in 1879 an excavated burial ground near Birdlip contained three skeletons, a large bronze bowl, and a decorated mirror. These early peoples moved about the hills, for old stones, guiding the way, have been found beside ancient tracks. Cromlechs to mark special spots used for religious rites, are dotted over the region. The old rocking stone at Buckston may have had Druidal connections. It was overturned by visitors in 1885, but has since been restored and cemented to its base.

When the Romans occupied England, one of their greatest military camps was at Cirencester, 'the capital of the Cotswolds'. They built villas on the slopes of the hills, with that at Chedworth being a typical example. On the warmer slopes they grew vines, and their imported edible snails are still to be found at Chedworth and elsewhere. Famous Roman roads which cross the Cotswolds are Fosse Way, going through Moreton-in-Marsh, Northleach, Cirencester and Bath, a mile to the east of Cirencester the Fosse is joined by Akeman Street, and in the town, Ermine Street crosses the Fosse.

The Saxons who settled in the Cotswolds after the Romans had left, cleared woods and set up self-supporting manors, as at Winchcombe, Coln Rogers, and Bibury. Saxon finds at Fairford and Avening include iron swords, lance heads, bronze brooches, rings, amulets and glass beads. The Normans took over the manorial system of the Saxons after 1066, and feudalised it. They built handsome churches in

Cotswold stone, established corn mills, and terraced hill-slopes for vines.

During the fifteenth century Cirencester became the chief centre of the wool trade. Chipping Campden and Northleach became collecting centres. Throughout the region, vast churches were built with the wealth accrued by wool merchants. Much wool was exported to Europe, but London merchants preferred Cotswold wool to any other. By the middle of the next century great tracts of Cotswold uplands were turned into sheep-walks, so displacing arable landworkers.

In the reign of Elizabeth I, great fairs were established at Cirencester, Stow-on-the-Wold, Winchcombe, Tetbury, Wotton-under-Edge, and Marshfield. Later, in 1646, the last battle of the Civil Wars took place at Stow-on-the-Wold, when the Parliamentarians won. Meanwhile, the cloth-trade grew, for there were streams to wash the wool, and deposits of Fuller's earth to de-grease fleeces. Woad for dyeing wool grew in profusion.

Much road-building took place in the Cotswolds during the eighteenth century, with gates and tolls erected under the new Turnpike Acts. Many tollhouses exist today, but only for living in.

Enclosures which brought about the chequerboard pattern of small fields with separating hedges or, as in the Cotswolds, with dry stone walls, were a feature of the eighteenth century. Over eighty parks were established, attached to manors or country houses, the largest being Earl Bathurst's estate near Cirencester. During the nineteenth century, the demand for wool decreased, and the cloth trade in the Cotswolds went into decline. As a result, the numbers of sheep of the true Cotswold breed gradually declined. The importation of white flour from America also spelled the end of much of the milling of home-grown wheat, and more of the arable land went back to grass.

In more recent times, with highly mechanised only a small force is required, so small towns and some villages in the region have embraced other kinds of employment, such as light industries, handicrafts, and that connected with tourism.

Trout farming has become important in the Cotswolds. The hatchery at Bibury was established in 1900, and others have arisen since then. Hundreds of thousands of rainbow and brown trout are either sold as ova, as graded fish for stocking ponds and reservoirs, or over the counter for home-cooking. Ova are also flown, packed in ice, to countries overseas where waters are regularly stocked.

These old picture postcards give an insight into Cotswold life between 1880 and 1930, and provide examples of its scenic beauty, lovely villages, and small towns.

Acknowledgements:

Acknowledgements with thanks are made to the following for their help with illustrations: 8, 16, 17, 19, 21, 22, 24, 25, 27, 33, 34, 36, 40, 46, 53, 55, 58, 59, 60, 62, 63, 65, 66, 69, 70, 71, 75, Mrs. F. Gittos; 56, The Cotswold Farm Park, Rare Breeds Survival Centre, Guiting Power; 38, Mr. H.W.G. Elwes of Colesbourne Park; the rest are from the author's collection of Victorian and Edwardian postcards. My thanks also to my wife for her help and interest.

Chipping Campden, High Street

1. Chipping Campden is a small town rather than a village. Most of its buildings are of Cotswold stone, and architecturally include canopied doorways, gables, and oriel windows. One of the finest houses is that of a rich wool merchant, William Grevel, which was built in the fourteenth century. Wool Staplers Hall, also of that period, was restored between 1902 and 1911. In 1902 a Guild of Craftsmen from London set up in Sheep Street premises to work at printing, book-binding, furniture making, wrought-iron work, and enamelling. Fine work in gold, silver and copper was also undertaken. Many craftsmen still work in Sheep Street, producing items in silver, iron and other materials. In 1929 the Campden Trust was formed. Properties in the High Street were bought and restored, so contributing to the preservation of the town's rich architecture. The postcard shows the main street as it was in 1927.

Campden Church 1490 A.D.

2. This view of the fifteenth century Perpendicular 'wool' church is dated 1910. The church, whose tower rises to a height of 120 feet, has accumulated many treasures over the centuries. Grevel, and others after him, contributed generously to its building. A brass inside describes Grevel as 'the flower of the wool merchants of all England'. A good deal of restoration of the church took place between 1875 and 1876, and in 1878 Hardman was responsible for the window over the chancel arch. A Gloucestershire craftsman, Henry Payne, put in the fine east window. It was finished about 1920 and commemorates the men of Campden who died in the Great War of 1914-1918. Adjacent to the church is one of the lodges of Campden House, built by Sir Baptist Hicks, in 1612. In 1645 the Royalist forces garrisoned there wantonly destroyed it. The town's old cart-wash is just below the railings.

17632. THE MARKET HALL. CHIPPING CAMPDEN ~ JUDGES LTD.

3. This is the old, stone-built and stone-tiled Market Hall at Chipping Campden, built by Sir Baptist Hicks in 1627. It was originally intended for the sale of butter, cheese, eggs and poultry, but other commodities gradually found a sale there. As is evident, the building has five open bays with semi-circular arches, two bays and two gables at each end, and columns down the middle. Such market halls, with many variations, are to be found in most Cotswold towns. The Hicks coat of arms is at one end, and the floor is of stone. The scene is in the 1920s, and marks the transition period between horse transport and that of the motor car. The horse-drawn float is parked whiie the milkman crosses the street to make a delivery. To do light shopping on horseback was not uncommon. The streets were lit by gas, and the hanging sign denotes the office of the Chipping Campden and District Gas Company.

J. JACQUES, JUNR., BROADWAY.

"THE FISH INN," BROADWAY HILL.

4. Fish Hill, between Chipping Campden and Broadway, is 600 feet above sea-level. Two quarries for Cotswold stone were worked here when this photograph of the inn was taken in 1906. One old site has been landscaped to provide car-parking space, picnic places, and a viewing point. Grass-sowing and tree-planting have transformed it into a green and pleasant place. Close by, isolated across the road, is the Fish Inn, built in 1771. It has an outside staircase built of stone, and the building still functions as an inn. Samuel Cotterell was the landlord in 1906, licensed to sell beer, wines and spirits. Recently, the old quarry adjoining the inn has been reopened, but a nearby graveyard for old cars has destroyed the scenic beauty towards which the faces of the people in the photograph are directed.

5. Beacon Hill, overlooking Broadway, had a fire-beacon station there in Napoleonic times. Broadway Tower, a stone structure 60 feet high, was built about 1800 by Earl Coventry, of Croome Court, Worcestershire. The Countess of Coventry was undecided whether she could see the summit of the hill, 1,047 feet, from Croome Court, so she arranged for a fire to be lit on it. As the outcome was successful, she persuaded the earl to build the tower. A spiral staircase in stone leads on to its flat roof, to bring into view a beautiful countryside of wolds, woodlands, farms, and snug villages. In the near distance, the Malvern, Lickey, and Clent hills are in view, as are the more distant eminences such as the Long Mynd and Clee Hills in Shropshire, and the Black Mountains in Wales. The tower has been lived in most of the time. Today, the public can ascend to the top to enjoy the wide prospect, for it has become part of a modern leisure park.

THE COTSWOLDS ABOVE BROADWAY.

6. This scenic view of the Cotswolds above Broadway was taken in 1927. Dry stone walls give the fields their boundaries, but they are now expensive to maintain and so, in some cases, have been removed. Ploughing is being done by tractor and by horses, marking the transition stage between the two methods. Early tractors were heavy, slow, and not always reliable, so farmers tended to keep their options open by retaining some horse power. However, with the speedy improvement in tractor performance, the horse was superseded completely. It is interesting to compare the same scene today for, in spite of reports to the contrary in many areas, more hedgerow trees and copses seem to have been planted here than in the past. The ground being ploughed is for wheat or barley, the two most widely-grown cereals in the Cotswolds whose acreage has increased greatly in recent years.

THE NORTH COTSWOLD HOUNDS ON BROADWAY GREEN.

7. Broadway, a village beloved by tourists, stands at the edge of the Cotswolds in the north, and adjacent to the fertile Vale of Evesham. Hunting has been a Cotswold pursuit for many centuries, the quarry being the stag and fox. Today it is confined to the fox. The hunting scene shown here was taken during the last year of Queen Victoria's reign. The accoutrements of the huntsmen and huntswomen were much the same then as they are today – hunting pink for the men's jackets, and black for the women. The long skirts of the women onlookers are typical of the period. Hunts, as they still do, attracted all kinds of followers. Then they were on foot, or in horse-drawn vehicles which stopped at vantage points along the roads. The hounds were under the control of the kennel-man, or 'whipper-in' as he was called when in the field. The Broadway Hotel overlooking the Green, and the Lygon Arms Hotel further up, were the meeting places most frequently used.

OLD CROSS, SAINTBURY,
NEAR BROADWAY.

8. The Old Cross at Saintbury stands alongside the main Broadway to Stratford road. It dates from about 1400, and is 11 feet high. Similar crosses are to be found in the majority of Cotswold villages. The shaft, with a cubed dial surmounted by a small Maltese cross, was added in 1850. A by-road leads to the village which is almost unique among Cotswold villages in that nearly every house is separated from its neighbour by twists in the hillside. Saintbury is pure Cotswold, with roofs steeply pitched to carry the weight of stone tiles, and to prevent snow lying on them. In 1910, the date of the postcard, cowsheds were under the same long roofs as the farmhouses to keep everything snug in the winter. The church above the village has a Saxon mass dial, but is otherwise Norman. A candelabrum of wrought-iron made by C.R. Ashbee of Chipping Campden, was installed in 1911.

The Village, Stanton

9. Architecturally, Stanton is a distinguished village, made up of late Tudor houses, cottages, and farmsteads, with its main street climbing a gentle hill slope to the Mount Inn. Built of durable Cotswold stone, with stone-slated, lichen-covered roofs, most of the houses have attractive gardens, many of which are open to the public once a year as a collective effort for a worthy cause. Stanton Court, a fine Jacobean house, was purchased in 1906 by Sir Philip Stott when most of the village belonged to the estate, but was rather run down. Sir Philip began a programme to restore farmhouses, cottages, and barns without spoiling their appearance, planned and built a reservoir in the hills, installed a sewage system and treatment works, and in 1910 constructed a public swimming pool. In the 1920s he installed well-designed electric street lamps, and also repaired the village cross with its mediaeval base and shaft, and seventeenth century sundial and globe.

10. Stanton church, photographed here in 1920, is late Norman to Perpendicular, with some nineteenth century rebuilding. Some mediaeval pews survive, and deep grooves in the ends of those at the back have been made by the leashes of shepherds' dogs over the centuries. John Wesley, the originator of Methodism, is said to have preached from the fine Jacobean pulpit. The rood screen and loft were the gift of Sir Philip Stott, and were installed in 1923. Lord Ismay, who had a distinguished war record as adviser to Sir Winston Churchill, was married here in 1921. The south-facing porch has a small room above it which houses a varied collection of agricultural implements and household utensils of the last century. There are several interesting table-tombs in the churchyard as well as the cross designed by Sir Ninian Comper as a village war memorial, and erected in 1919.

11. Snowshill appears to be rooted on the hillside from which the stone of its buildings was quarried. When approached from Broadway, there are grand views over Evesham Vale, the Malvern Hills, and the immediate neighbourhood. While the 1928 view shown here may suggest an unchanging village, four cottages were converted in 1925 into a single unit, and others have since been similarly modified and updated. A few new houses have been built in stone to maintain the character of the place. The most fascinating building is the sixteenth century Manor House which has successively belonged to abbots and royalty. When it was bought in 1919 by the scholar and architect Charles Wade, it was being used as a farmhouse. He restored it, and in 1951 gave it to the National Trust. It is now a museum of Mr. Wade's collections, which include musical instruments, models of English counties farm waggons, penny-farthing bicycles, clocks, dolls and eastern scrolls.

Val Doone.]   [*Richmond.*

SNOWSHILL.

DUMBLETON CHURCH & FOUNTAIN, GLOS.

12. The carrier with his horse and light waggon, 1905, has come from Buckland, a neighbouring village. He gained a living by collecting and delivering parcels and commodities throughout the district. The stone trough of the fountain held water for horses, and parishioners filled their buckets from the spout at the front. Though no longer in use, the fountain makes a charming focal point in a grassy setting. The church is mainly Norman, with later additions. Its interior is extremely rich in carvings. Through the fourteenth century chancel arch is a fine monument to Charles Percy, a sixteenth century knight in armour, with his family. The pulpit with its panels of carved fruits, and the south porch with its sundial, were provided in 1905. Altogether, Dumbleton is a village of lovely old cottages and fine houses, with extensive views of the Cotswolds. Dumbleton mill, eighteenth century, on the river Isbourne, still has its machinery in situ.

In Bredon Village.

ARTHUR WILKES, Post Office, Bredon.

13. To take the main Evesham road from Dumbleton and turn left for Beckford is to enter an outlying area whose villages are in the Cotswold tradition to a large extent. Thus, Beckford, Overbury, Kemerton, Bredon, Bredon's Norton, Great and Little Comberton, Elmley Castle, Ashton-under-Hill and Conderton are all villages of character. Bredon has grown extensively, but in the older parts, thatch, brick tiles, and Welsh slates, have been used for roofing, as well as Cotswold stone slates. The postcard shows that dry stone walls for garden boundaries were of a high standard of construction. The church and the enormous tithe barn nearby are the gems of Bredon. Donkey transport in this 1907 scene was common in this region which has short hills and narrow lanes. The slow pace of donkeys was suited to the times. They took families to church or chapel, on visits to friends and relatives, and on shopping expeditions.

STANWAY HOUSE.

14. The postcard of Stanway House and gatehouse is dated 1907. Both buildings are faced with square hewn stone known as ashlar. The estate originally belonged to Tewkesbury monastery, but was acquired by the Tracy family in the sixteenth century. They built the present house round about 1600, and from them it descended to the Earl of Wemyss. Unlike most manor houses, it is L-shaped, with a huge bay window. The gatehouse, 1630, is probably the work of a Cotswold master-mason. Beautifully proportioned, it has several embellishments, including the Tracy scallops. Under a tulip tree in the grounds, King Edward VII was guest at a tea-party in 1904. On Open Days, the house, tithe barn, church, and immediate area, are worth exploring. A cricket pavilion, on the opposite side of the road, was built by Sir James Barrie, the author of Peter Pan, a play which holds its charm for children today.

OLD TYTHE BARN, STANWAY

15. The tithe barn at Stanway was built in the fourteenth century for the abbot of Tewkesbury, and is one of the oldest in England. It has huge buttresses and massive timbers, and stands within the grounds of Stanway House. Shown here as it was in 1898, it is typical of many such barns in the Cotswolds, as at Hampnett, Postlip Hall, and Syde. The expansive roof shows how the slates were laid – large ones at the eaves and graded upwards to small ones at the ridge – the traditional way for this kind of roofing. Such an enormous weight is supported by cruck frames embedded in the thick walls. The barn was repaired in 1925, and since then has been used as a hall for all kinds of district occasions, such as flower and vegetable shows, art and craft exhibitions, theatrical performances by local amateur companies and touring companies of professional actors, music concerts, and lectures.

Gloucester Street, Winchcombe.
Vicarage on the right.

16. Winchcombe, in the valley of the Isbourne, was a walled town in Saxon times. This 1905 view shows how the stone houses form an unbroken line along Gloucester Street. The houses and carts, and the girls in their white pinafores, typify the early Edwardian era, before motor cars had made their appearance in great numbers. Towering above the town is the enormous 'wool' church, dating from about 1465, and bearing witness to the fact that five-hundred clothiers worked here during the fifteenth century. Some forty gargoyles, an altar cloth made by Catherine of Aragon, and the giant wooden, gilded weather-cock brought from St. Mary Redcliffe, Bristol, in 1872, are among the many interesting features of the church. At almost 1,000 feet among the hills to the south of the town is Belas Knap, a famous New Stone Age long barrow with four, stone-lined burial chambers. The views all round are magnificent.

High Street. Winchcombe.

17. This 1902 view of Winchcombe High Street portrays several features which typify the late Victorian era. Horse-drawn vehicles with their passengers could be accommodated at the White Hart, on the right, and so could the few motorists as yet on the roads. Cycling for men and women was a craze, and billiard saloons were common. The White Hart functions as a hotel today. The low-gabled house next door is timber-framed, and of the sixteenth century. It has been modified inside, and is now an eating place known as the Wesley Restaurant. Beyond the three-storeyed building is a pre-Reformation timber-framed building, the George Hotel, once an inn for pilgrims to Winchcombe Abbey, and to Hailes Abbey, a mile or so away. The Winchcombe Town Hall clock, on the left, was the gift of Reginald Prance, of Hampstead, London, in 1897, to mark Queen Victoria's Jubilee. Many other houses have been transformed into family shops of various kinds.

ABBEY TERRACE AND HIGH STREET, WINCHCOMBE.

18. This view of Abbey Terrace and High Street, Winchcombe, will revive memories among older people of the series of warm summers of the Edwardian era, when picnics, driving in open horse-drawn carriages, and bicycling, were the pastimes of the well-to-do. The dress of the women and children, the raised sun-blinds over the shop fronts, and the clear sky, all point to settled weather. Abbey Terrace, seen here in 1906, is so-called because a great Benedictine Abbey, of which there is now little trace, once stood in the area to the left behind the trees. The middle building facing the Square is now Lloyds Bank, while among the others are doctors' surgeries and solicitors' offices. The space in which the women are standing is now a car park, with standing for coaches and local buses. Even so, the town is quieter than many places of comparable size, for it is not on a main highway.

Cheltenham Promenade

19. Cheltenham, mostly a Georgian spa town, advertises itself as 'The Gateway to the Cotswolds'. With ample hotel and other accommodation it is a good centre in which to stay, for on its north-east side is the immense amphitheatre of the Cotswold escarpment. The promenade, as seen above in the 1920s, was, and still is, a busy thoroughfare. On the left is a row of high-class shops, and on the right are the post office, more shops, and the Municipal Offices. The wide road is skirted with trees, and in front of the Municipal Offices are seats, lawns, and flower beds. There is also a Memorial to the dead of the First World War, a bronze statue of Wilson, the Cheltonian who died with Scott on his ill-fated expedition to the South Pole in 1912, and the Neptune Fountain. Apart from the bull-nosed Morris cars by the shops, a popular way of getting around was on a bicycle, for in the town there are no big hills.

Cheltenham from Devil's Chimney

20. Leckhampton Hill lies to the south of Cheltenham, and for centuries tourists have made the journey to its top to view the extensive panorama over to the west. Besides commanding a spectacular view of Cheltenham, on a clear day the Forest of Dean, the Severn Plain, and the mountains of mid-Wales can be seen. The spires of several cathedrals and churches can be picked out by anyone interested in details. From the summit, not far away, stands the detached rock known as 'The Devil's Chimney'. It was probably left behind during quarrying operations all round it. The postcard, 1928, gives a good view of Cheltenham itself. Many years ago experienced climbers used to scale the rock as a challenge, but there were occasions when less skilled ones became stranded at the top. Rescuing them was a difficult task. Today, the stones which form this precipitous rock are in a crumbling condition, so to attempt to climb it would be foolhardy.

21. Leckhampton Hill has been extensively quarried in times past, and some of the now abandoned quarries can be seen in the background of this mid-1920s postcard. The electric tramcar service was begun in 1899, causing the previous horse-bus service to close down by 1903. Cheltonians and visitors joined the tram at St. James' Square, and got out at the Malvern Inn, Leckhampton. Running up the hill on the right is the old railway track which was the route along which good quality Cotswold stone was brought in trucks from the quarries to the main road. Here it was off-loaded on to horse-drawn waggons and, later, on to steam-driven lorries. These were quickly superseded by motor lorries, and the quarrying ceased round about 1928. The tram service flourished between 1906 and 1930, with the exception of the war years, but the advent of the motor bus led to the closure of the trams in 1930.

22. Another magnificent scenic view, this time to the north of Cheltenham, is to be had from the top of Cleeve Hill, at over 1,000 feet. When the first electric tram service was introduced in 1899, the 3ft. 6in. gauge line, six miles long from its depot at Lansdown, was among the first to be constructed. The work of installing the track and overhead cables began at Cleeve Hill, and proceeded downwards into Cheltenham. Passing-loops were made at intervals as it was a single line. The overturning of a tram on the downward run in July 1901, shortly after the service had begun, killing two workmen, shook public confidence for a while. Prosperity soon came to the hill, however, for the 'Rising Sun' doubled its size, and cafés sprang up to cater for the crowds. The tramway itself also prospered, but was inevitably superseded by the motor omnibus. It closed down in 1930, but many people still have happy memories of its thirty years of service.

A Corner of Bishop's Cleeve.

23. Lying below Cleeve Hill is Bishop's Cleeve, a village with a twelfth century church which is a notable landmark for miles around. The scene, 1909, of boys playing marbles, was photographed before the street surface was macadamised. Marbles is a seasonal game which most people will have played when they were young. Bowling marbles to and from school was one way of enjoying the journeys if they were over long distances. The boys here are playing the simple traditional game of hitting an opponent's marble by flicking his own at it. There were also more complicated ways of playing, with a hole scraped in the ground, and the use of a pitcher (a small piece of slate) to hit marbles which escaped the hole when they were 'laid'. Today, this same street is continuously busy with motor traffic. Bishop's Cleeve has a mixed architecture. There are dry stone walls, stone houses with Cotswold roofing slates, thatched houses, and brick buildings.

"Seven Springs" (Source of the Thames), Near Cheltenham Spa.

12938.

24. At Coberley, near Cheltenham Spa, is a wayside feature known as Seven Springs. Controversy has long reigned, especially in 1923, as to whether the spot really marks the source of the Thames, for Thames Head, at Kemble, near Cirencester, also makes the claim. Modern tourist maps differentiate between the two by marking the former as the 'Rival' source of the Thames, and the latter merely as the source. A statement in the House of Commons in 1937 stated that Thames Head was officially the true source. At Seven Springs, a Latin hexameter, signed T.S.E., and fixed to the back wall, can just be seen in this 1928 postcard. It reads 'Hic tuus O Tamisine Pater Septemgeminus fons'. The springs used to gush with force, but this is not so today, although there is a constant pool of clear water beneath the wall. In the 1900s they constituted a favourite spot for a picnic outing as there was a good pull-off for horse vehicles.

Painswick. New Street.

25. Painswick is a small town set on a well-wooded spur of the Cotswold Hills. New Street above, at the turn of the century, is the main through-road from Cheltenham to Stroud. The Falcon Hotel, with its notable bowling green, is on the right, and the boy holding the pony is earning a penny while the owner has a drink. The many roads which open off New Street and the church area are bordered by historic buildings dating from the sixteenth to nineteenth centuries. There are turnpike houses, roundhouses, an old brewery, and several old mill sites along the river valleys just outside the town. Today, Painswick caters for tourists and, in August, at the Institute Club, holds an annual Exhibition of the Guild of Gloucestershire Craftsmen. Here, furniture, pottery, engraved glass, carved wood, stained-glass, book-binding, embroidery, jewellery, weaving, silk-screen printing, and other craftwares are displayed. Picture galleries and antique shops, as well as bookshops, add to the interest of the town.

PAINSWICK CHURCH

26. Painswick church is mainly of the sixteenth century in style, and has one of the most striking spires in the Cotswolds. The first spire was destroyed by lightning in 1883, and the present one was built with the whitish oolite, known as Painswick stone, dug from a local quarry. The south vestry was built in 1890, and several windows date between 1880 and 1925. There are twelve bells, all retuned and reframed between 1899 and 1900. The Ancient Society of Painswick Youths was founded in 1686 to promote bell-ringing, an art which has brought many record peals to Painswick over the years, and continues today. The church-yard is famous for its many decorated table-tombs, as well as for its avenues of clipped yews. Some of the latter were first planted in 1794. Over the years the accounts of their number have varied from exactly ninety-nine, to over one hundred. Whatever the case, they are most impressive.

27. In the sixteenth century, Huguenot refugees settled in Stroud, and established the cloth-making industry. All the ingredients for success were there – Cotswold wool, a constant supply of water from the Frome, spring water for cleaning and dyeing the wool and, in the nineteenth century, canals and railway for transport. The Frome valley had almost two-hundred cloth-mills in 1824. They produced high quality cloth for military uniforms, hunting 'pink', billiard tables, and tennis balls. When the mills had to close, new light engineering and other industries kept Stroud in a relatively prosperous state. This 1908 postcard shows the town to be alive with horse traffic. Off the Parade, streets are narrow and winding, with warehouses, workshops, houses, chapels, shops and inns, crowded upon each other. The School of Science and Art was established in 1890.

Seven Springs, Bisley

28. From time immemorial the springs at Bisley, near Stroud, have gushed out from the hillside into a narrow lane below the church. Between 1862 and 1864, the rector, Thomas Keble, restored both the church and springs. The latter were made to run out of five recesses in a stone wall, and out of two small spouts lower down into two stone water-troughs. It is said that in mediaeval times the springs supplied the bath water for monks. Until the 1930s, the villagers used the spring water for drinking and other household purposes. When the mains-water was installed round about 1940, they fell into disuse. An Ascension Day church service, with a procession of children carrying flowers to decorate the springs, has been a centuries-old custom. There is an old lock-up in the centre of the village, and Stancombe toll-house, a mile north-west of this, is a two-storey building in good condition, and now a dwelling house.

View at Uley.

29. As this view of 1923 shows, Uley is a village set among hills and trees. The many lovely cottages and houses built over several centuries are in harmony with each other, and express the Cotswold tradition of building. Some houses have hipped roofs, that is, roofs which slope at their ends instead of being vertical. The church in the background was rebuilt in 1858 after the former one had been destroyed twenty years earlier. A monument in the tower informs us that John Eyles was the first man to make Spanish cloth in the parish during the late seventeenth century. A mile from the church is the famous Hetty Pegler's Tump, a long barrow 120 feet long and 90 feet wide, with an excavated gallery of massive stones and two side chambers. It is open to the public. Half a mile away is Uleybury, an Iron Age fort enclosing thirty-two acres. From its top extensive views may be had over a rolling countryside.

The Marsh Mills, Uley.

30. This old cloth mill was engaged in making broadcloth at Uley two centuries ago. The village was famous for 'Uley Blues', a blue cloth produced by dyeing with a mixture of weld and indigo. The weld came from local sources. With the movement of the cloth trade to Yorkshire, however, the industry in Uley declined, and the closure of Marsh Mill in 1837, along with others, brought it to an end. This 1905 postcard shows the mill largely unaltered. Its louvered upper storeys were the drying rooms for the wool. Over the years the waterwheels and machinery fell into decay and were removed. The site became a timber-yard, and the old drying rooms became ideal for air-drying stored timber. In more recent years, the mill has been converted into a house, and the acreage around it to farming on the organic system. The restored water-course, with its wildlife, is also an attractive feature.

Town Hall,   Tetbury.

31. At Tetbury, all roads lead to the Town or Market Hall. The Tetbury Rural District Council Offices, however, are in Long Street, whose houses show the various stages of Cotswold domestic architecture over many centuries. The Market Hall was built in 1655, and altered in 1817 to look like this postcard view of 1905. The open south end was enclosed for storage purposes. The original purpose of the Hall was a collecting centre for the weighing of wool. Its fat Tuscan pillars of stone present a massive appearance to the bays. A smaller market or Tolsey in Chipping Street was concerned with the weighing and selling of cheeses and bacon. Tetbury's church, whose spire just protrudes above the roof of the Hall from behind, was rebuilt in 1787, and the tower and spire between 1890 and 1893. The old Brewery in the town is an industrial monument, architecturally, and was connected with the railway before it was closed down in the 1960s.

Old Pike House, Bath Road, Tetbury.

32. Tetbury is the meeting place of five important roads, and names such as Old Pike House, seen here in 1904, help to identify exactly where road tolls were collected by the agents of the Turnpike Companies during the nineteenth century. Many such houses are still to be seen throughout the Cotswolds. The collectors lived in them, and had to be available at all hours to let travellers through. Toll houses commanded a shape wholly their own, either octagonal or round, so that windows or apertures in the walls would give a view of the roads from all directions. Travelling by stage-coach was common throughout the nineteenth century, and reached its hey-day between 1820 and 1836, just before the railway system began to affect the takings at toll gates. By 1879 very few of the latter were left in Gloucestershire. From Tetbury to Dursley, less than ten miles, the toll was 1s. 6d. for a horse and trap. This was regarded as high.

Canal Tunnel, Sapperton.

33. This is the Sapperton entrance to the Thames and Severn Canal, as it was in 1906. Built between 1784 and 1789, it is over two miles long, and the tunnel bore is fifteen feet high and fourteen feet wide. The arch at this end was given an embattled parapet. The other end, at Coates, is more ornate, with two niches for statues. On 20 April 1789 the first barge went through, and the last on 11 May 1911. The bargees propelled their craft through the tunnel by lying on their backs on the decks and pushing with their feet against the roof or walls. Known as 'leggers', they were able to quench their thirst at the Tunnel House inn, at Coates, and at the Bricklayers' Arms, now renamed the Daneway Inn, at the Sapperton end. The tunnel had problems with water leaking through the porous limestone, so fresh supplies had to be pumped by a windmill at Thames Head. In due course, engines took over the pumping, but ceased altogether in 1927.

Cirencester Church

34. In Roman times, Cirencester, or Corinium as it was then called, was the focal point of three great highways, Ermine Street, Akeman Street, and the Fosse Way. The town's Corinium Museum houses many exhibits of the Roman occupation. The fifteenth century parish church is one of the finest in England, and larger than some of our cathedrals. It bears witness to the prosperity of the town in the heyday of the Cotswold wool industry. This scene, 1908, shows the unique, sixteenth century, three-storeyed porch which, from 1672 onwards was used as a Town Hall until the building of new municipal offices in Castle Street. Opposite the church, behind where the waggons of grain are waiting, is the Market Place where great sheep fairs used to be held. However, with the coming of the railway, a new market was set up in 1867 off Tetbury Road, close to the station. Marketing of vegetables, fruits, and other products still take place at the old market on market days, Monday and Friday.

A Peep in the Park, Cirencester

35. Cirencester Park was the work of Allen, the first Lord Bathurst (1684-1775). He enclosed some 3,000 acres of what had been open, uncultivated downland, and landscaped it according to his own ideas and in consultation with his literary friend and poet, Alexander Pope. The tree-planting which he carried out resulted in the park which has often been described as the English Versailles, and is regarded as one of the finest in the country. Its spine is the Broad Avenue, fifty yards wide, which stretches five miles or so. To walk along it up to a shelter known as Pope's seat, and then to look back is to get a view of the church tower in all its magnificence. As this 1906 postcard shows, there are many avenues of trees along which the public may freely walk. It is interesting to compare the avenues of beeches above with their maturity today. If anything, they are even more beautiful, and the whole park is full of wonders. The park was made available to the people of Cirencester in 1898.

Deer in Cirencester Park.

36. The Cotswolds have long been connected with hunting, coursing, and hawking. Wild stag hunting was one of the chief sports in Shakespeare's time, and lasted until the present century in areas which had good wood cover. Now only fox-hunting and beagling are the chief sports. Many of the great landowners who laid out their parks during the eighteenth century incorporated into them a tightly enclosed section usually referred to as the Deer Park. Some still remain within the Cotswolds. Deer were kept mainly for ornamental purposes, with an annual cull to provide venison for the table. Roe and fallow deer were the species most favoured, though a few herds of red deer were preferred by some landowners. The old Deer Park within Cirencester Park no longer contains these animals, pictured here in 1927, for it has been given over to educational purposes. Nevertheless, a wild deer may occasionally be seen among the glades.

37. According to Marshall in 'The Rural Economy of Gloucestershire', 1796, the use of oxen for ploughing was on the increase. They were harnessed like horses, with collar and hames, as above, 1912. Marshall noted that they began work at four years of age, and were kept on until the end of their sixth year, when they were fattened and sold. Oxen were suited to the light shallow soils of the higher Cotswolds, but horses were preferred on the heavy clay soils of the vales. This was because oxen 'poached' (trod) the soil too heavily. Arthur Gibbs, in 'A Cotswold Village', 1898, noted that oxen were rapidly being superseded by horses. By 1912 an oxen plough-team was a rarity, though on the Springhill Estate near Broadway teams were used until 1920. One was also kept on the Bathurst Estate at Cirencester until 1964 as a link with the past. Specimens of these great beasts can now be seen at the Cotswold Farm Park, Guiting Power.

38. Henry J. Elwes (1846-1922), of Colesbourne, became one of Britain's foremost authorities on trees and rare plants. After five years with the Scots Guards, in 1870 he took up the study of botany, zoology, and ornithology. He employed his time in travel, sport, and hunting for rare plants and animals in China, Japan, Siberia, Russia, Tibet, Turkey, and the Americas. Some ninety-eight specimens of plants which he introduced into the country were drawn and described in the Botanical Magazine. Among them were various species of snowdrops, fritillaries, crocuses, oxalis and primulas. In appreciation, some were named after him, as for example, the snowdrop Galanthus elwesii. He corresponded with the most eminent botanists of his time. His fame lies also in his seven-volume book, 'The Trees of Great Britain and Ireland', written between 1906 and 1913 in collaboration with Professor Augustine Henry, a notable botanist.

Colesbourne House

39. Colesbourne House was built in 1854 in the Jacobean style to the design of David Brandon. It was pulled down in 1960, and replaced by a house more in keeping with modern needs. The bridge over the river Churn remains. The postcard of 1905 shows the old house standing in attractive grounds, for the estate covered an extensive area round about, hilly and well-wooded. Much of the mature woodland that exists today is due to the work and foresight of Henry J. Elwes who moved into the house in 1890 on the death of his father. In addition to planting some 800 acres of woods on the poorer hill soil, he established an arboretum in the vicinity of the house and church. The many rare trees include cut-leaf mountain ash, Californian nutmeg, cut-leaf hazel, Japanese wingnut, rare limes, Siberian elm, Turkish hazel, and the golden western red cedar. The collection is still being added to by his great-grandson, H.W.G. Elwes.

The Square, Bibury

40. Bibury is a scattered village with interesting features at various points within it. The main part is centred round The Square, as above in 1909. It is to the north-west of the church, and is composed of very fine seventeenth and eighteenth century cottages built in the Cotswold tradition. One carries a carved tablet with the date 1769. William Morris described Bibury in 1870 as the most beautiful village in England, surrounded as it is by the Cotswold Hills, and the river Coln flowing through it. The present church was built on the foundations of a Saxon church by the Normans, and there are additions dating from the fourteenth and fifteenth centuries. Some of the glass windows and interior furnishings are nineteenth century. Bibury Court, by the Coln, is largely Jacobean, but its interior was remodelled in 1922 and the building is now a hotel. Nearby is the Old Vicarage, behind it the fifteenth century Pigeon House, and a round dovecote.

The Swan Hotel, BIBURY

41. The Swan Hotel, overlooking the Coln, has accommodated anglers for a century or more, for the cold, clear waters of the river have always been famous for their trout. No doubt the sightseers who have disembarked from the horse-drawn carriage, used at the turn of the century for touring the district, are looking over the bridge wall in the hope of spotting a good trout facing upstream. The three-arched bridge was built in 1779. The hotel has attractive gardens, and in 1900 a spring within them was estimated to feed some two million gallons of water into the Coln every day. A large number of mallard and other ornamental duck inhabit the river and its banks, and form part of the wild-life which attracts visitors from far and wide. The latter now come by motor coaches in larger numbers than could ever have been brought by the horse-drawn carriage above. Nevertheless, the village is still largely unspoilt.

View from Swan Hotel, Bibury.

42. Within view of the Swan Hotel is Arlington Mill, built in the seventeenth century as a cloth mill, and later converted into a corn mill. It is now a folk museum and art gallery. Just before this postcard was made, 1902, a trout farm was established on the ground to the right of the stream leading to the mill. It is now run on commercial lines, with many acres of ponds, and thousands of fish graded in pens according to size. They are also marketed as frozen ova and sent by air to stock rivers in other countries. Brown trout, in the wild, can reach nine pounds in weight, but at the farm are sold at about three pounds. Rainbow trout grow faster, to reach about six pounds in weight. The brown trout is very territorial in rivers, but the rainbow trout is not, and so is well-suited for ponds and lakes. The farm attracts large numbers of visitors who delight in seeing the fish being fed, or in buying freshly prepared specimens for the table.

43. Arlington Row, Bibury, comprises a world-famous group of grey walled, grey roofed, and gabled cottages. They were built in the fourteenth century as a wool store, and were converted into cottages for weavers in the seventeenth century when Arlington Mill, only a stone's throw away, was a cloth mill. Wool was spread on drying racks in the field behind the cottages which now goes by the name of Rack Isle. The row is aesthetically attractive because of the varying architectural features found in it, and because of the extensive reach of the roof tiling. Each cottage has something to contribute to a harmonious whole, almost as if it had always existed beside the adjoining stream and against the background of gentle well-wooded hills. The row was bought and repaired by the Royal Society of Arts in 1929, and upkeep is in the hands of the National Trust.

COLN ST. ALDWYN'S, GLOS. POST OFFICE &c.

TAUNT'S SERIES 1836

44. One of the most beautiful valleys in England is that of the river Coln. Three villages bearing that name are there – Coln Rogers, Coln St. Dennis, and Coln St. Aldwyns. The postcard is dated 1906. The whole area is well-wooded. Coln St. Aldwyns has a fine Elizabethan manor house which, originally, was a farmhouse, but was altered in 1896, enlarged, and turned into the country residence of Sir Michael Hicks-Beach, then Chancellor of the Exchequer. His arms are over the main door. The church, basically Norman, has later additions, and some restoration was undertaken in 1853. The chancel was refurbished in 1916 in memory of the first Earl St. Aldwyn. John Keble, poet and divine (1792-1866), was curate to his father from 1825 to 1835. He composed hymns which are sung in churches today, and he was also author of 'The Christian Year'. The glass in two lancets of the chancel was added in 1910 to their memory.

W. D. M. & CO.   0184.

High Street, Fairford.

45. Fairford, also on the river Coln, is almost a small town. The High Street leads to the Market Place, and nearly all its grey stone houses date from the seventeenth and eighteenth centuries. The dress of the children dates the postcard as Victorian. The horse-drawn farm tumbril contains a crate for transporting either pigs, sheep, or calves to the butcher or market. A loaded carrier's waggon stands at the far end of the street. Fairford church is famous for its twenty-eight mediaeval windows of stained glass, the gift of John Tame, a rich wool merchant who rebuilt the church between 1480 and 1500. The glass was probably the work of British and Flemish glaziers. It tells the bible story from Eden to the Crucifixion, and from the time of the Apostles to the Last Judgement. Some of the windows were re-leaded in 1889 after storm damage.

46. The demand for better means of transport in the Cotswolds, especially where villages and small towns were not close enough to the railway system, gradually led to the introduction of local omnibus services. The year 1904 saw the first omnibus service between Fairford and Cirencester, and this proved to be a great boon. The Cirencester and District Motor Omnibus Company's vehicle shown here had a driver and ticket collector. Its movable place-indicator board reads: 'Cirencester, Fairford, and Lechlade.' It served small villages in between at particular stopping places en route. Or individuals could board it anywhere by simply waving it to a halt. The frequency of a service was partly determined by market days. Goods and luggage were placed within the roof-rack, access to which was reached by means of the ladder carried behind the vehicle. The tarpaulin sheet was used to cover them in wet weather.

47. Ablington Manor was the home of J. Arthur Gibbs whose book, 'A Cotswold Village', (1898), was one of the first and finest books on the region. In many ways it can be regarded as a social document of his times. Such was its popularity that between 1898 and 1912 it was re-printed ten times. Gibbs gained all his pleasure in life from the old manor set in seclusion among the trees, and from everything that the Coln valley had to offer. He loved the outdoor life and sports, had a scholarly taste for literature, and was a discerning naturalist. His interest in people led him to play an active role in village life, in which cricket and fly-fishing formed a part. People in all walks of life regarded him as a friend. He had a fund of humorous stories, and was a past master at producing verses in the Gloucestershire dialect. Two months after his return from a holiday in Italy in March 1899, he died. He was only thirty-one.

48. As a naturalist and expert dry-fly fisherman, Gibbs knew the habits of trout in the Coln better than most. In his book he describes how, in early June, the fish rise to mayflies in mid-stream. Anglers try to deceive the trout by using artificial flies. Gibbs noted that the older and larger trout were very wily, and anglers tended to catch the less wary, smaller specimens, weighing under a pound. The photograph shows a morning's catch by the vicar of Fairford in 1910, at nearly eighteen pounds. Before and after 1900, fishermen were attracted to Fairford, and stayed at the Bull Hotel, itself widely known as the centre of the fishing. The season ran from 1 April to the end of September, and the landlord rented 1½ miles of the Coln, charging his guests 2s. 6d. per day to fish. Cotswold rivers and streams are still fished for trout, but trout farming has developed as a substantial industry throughout the region from 1900 to the present day.

49. Ablington is a beautiful hamlet of Bibury, and has no church of its own. The river Coln, depicted here in 1914, is attractively bridged, and flows on to Bibury. Just round the corner is a row of large stone cottages overlooking the road from a terrace. Below, in a stone wall, is a drinking fountain fashioned as a war memorial. Also very striking is one of three great barns, which, although built for the secular purpose of storing grain in its five bays, is almost cathedral-like in size and dignity. To the south of the hamlet is an Iron Age hill fort covering about nine acres, and known in 1824 as Rowbarrow Camp. To the right of the photograph, out of sight behind a wall and the tall trees, is Ablington Manor, built in the reign of Elizabeth I. An inscription on the porch says: 'Plead Thou my cause O Lord, by John Coxwell Ano Domeney 1590.' As has been said, Gibbs lived here.

50. The postcard shows a typical Cotswold landworker and his wife outside their cottage about 1897. His hours, before his retirement, had been long, the work hard, and the wage small. To be off work through illness was a threat to their livelihood. However, they lived through a period of quiet and seeming continuity, for changes were slow in coming. There were four occasions when farmers gave their men a feast. They were the Sower's feast, at the end of April; the Sheepshearer's feast, a boisterous affair; the Reaper's feast in August; and the Harvest Home in September. By 1900, the first three had largely been given up. The religious Harvest Festival took place in September in the church which was decorated with flowers and fruits. The old man, with his father before him, had lived in their cottage for eighty-six years. He and his wife had barely gone more than a few miles from the village during their lifetime.

51. Kelmscott Manor, on the Oxfordshire fringe of the Cotswolds, was the home of William Morris, famous as a poet, artist, craftsman and writer. He viewed factory-made goods as a degradation in taste, and started a movement for craftsman-made articles. He inspired others, such as Rossetti, Burne Jones, and Philip Webb to join him, and over many years they produced stained glass, tapestries, printed and woven hangings, furniture and wallpapers. Morris bought Kelmscott in 1871, and Rosetti took up residence as well. Design work, weaving, painting, poetry and prose emanated from the manor in volume. In 1890 Morris established a printing works at Hammersmith, and called it the Kelmscott Press. He died in 1896 and was buried at Kelmscott. A number of rooms furnished by him have been preserved at the Manor House which is open to visitors at arranged times. Four memorial cottages were built in the village in 1902 and 1915.

BURFORD.

52. Burford's houses in the sloping High Street stand shoulder to shoulder in an array of different architectural styles. The forest of Wychwood nearby provided the oak for the sixteenth century timber-framed houses which nestle among those built of stone. Over the years, many of them have been altered to serve as shops, and to cater for tourists, the antique furniture trade, and book businesses. Burford did not have a railway, but as it is on road routes leading to many other Cotswold towns, it developed a prosperous stage-coach trade during the eighteenth and nineteenth centuries. It still has the old coaching inns which have been modernised in keeping with their traditions, as well as hotels and restaurants. The cars in the street, of 1930 vintage, are now museum pieces. Today the street is usually very busy, but car-parking has been organised along both sides, and in free parks.

Burford Pageant—Her Highness Queen Elizabeth and Guard.

FOSTER, PHOTO.

PACKER, PRINTER.

53. In 1574 Queen Elizabeth I came through Burford from Langley on the occasion of a progress to show herself to her subjects. The visit was recorded as follows: *The Thewsday being the iij day of August the Queenes maiestye came from Langley throughe the towne of Burforde, where shee was resevyd at the bridge by the Bayllyffes, then beinge Rycharde Reynoldes and Rychard Chadwell, and Symon Wysdome Aldermane, with all the Burges of the same towne, presentinge her grace with a purse of gowlde, and xxᵗⁱ Aungells in the same purse. Offycers feys gyven at the charges of the whole towne as followethe: To the Clarke of the markett xxvjs iijd. To the Seargaunte of the Armes xiijs iiijd. To the Queene's footemen xxs. To the Trumpetors xiijs iiijd. To the Yeoman of the bottells, vjs. viiijd. God save the Queene.* From time to time since 1900 the town has held a pageant, such as the one above, to mark the occasion.

Will F. Taylor.]

[London.

NORTHLEACH.

54. Northleach, on the river Leach, is a small market town midway between Burford and Cirencester. As this 1927 postcard shows, the town is dominated by its massive church whose unique interior contains many fifteenth century brasses which commemmorate the wool merchants buried in the nave. Among them is John Forty, who built the nave in 1400, and died in 1458. The brasses depict sheep and sacks of wool, and the rich wool-staplers. The church was thoroughly restored in 1884. It is said to possess the most beautiful porch in all England. A long irregular street runs through the town, and now carries motor traffic plying between Cheltenham, Oxford and London. The Market Place is to one side of the road. Near the church are a large barn and fine pigeon house. The Old Grammar School is now the Rural District Council Office, a new school having been built in 1927.

MARKET PLACE, NORTHLEACH.

55. The Market Place, Northleach, seen here in the 1920s with its prominently sited war memorial, looks quiet and peaceful. The parked cars had not yet had to vie for a place in which to park. Both are open tourers, fashionable at the time, and the one by the ladder is a bull-nosed Morris two-seater with a rear 'dickie'. Billie's café served the needs of visitors and locals alike. Most of the old houses of Northleach are built of stone, quarried locally, but a few timber-framed buildings are to be found as well. One house round the corner by the ladder had no windows and was known as the Blind House. It was used as a lock-up, and still has its stone ceiling and rough wooden bed. There was also a Bridewell with a treadmill just outside the town. It is now a museum of very great interest. The timber-framed building beside Billie's café is the Sherborne Arms, and the post office, Ox-house restaurant, and a pharmacy are on the right where the two children are standing.

56. It is appropriate to include a postcard of a Cotswold sheep of the 'lion' breed because the 'wool' churches of the region owe their existence to the wealth which the wool of this animal provided. It is a large breed, up to 224 pounds in weight, with a leg of mutton at 30 pounds. The coarse, white wool was suitable for the making of heavy cloth. Flocks were folded on turnips and, later, on kale, and this helped to improve the fertility of the light upland soils. From the 1860s onwards urban housewives required smaller joints, so smaller breeds of grass-fed sheep were introduced, and as a consequence the numbers of the Cotswold breed declined. In 1850, 5,000 Cotswold rams were sold in Gloucester market, 4,000 in 1860, and by 1892 only 45 flocks remained. These dwindled to 19 in 1914, and to 8 in 1922. Today, a small flock can be seen at the Rare Breeds Survival Centre (Cotswold Farm Park), near Guiting Power.

57. Burton-on-the-Water, the water being the river Windrush, was sometimes described as 'the Venice of the Cotswolds'. It has low footbridges over the river similar to the one shown here, and both banks have broad greens, with trees, and houses further back. Many of the latter have been altered for commercial purposes as the town is highly geared to tourism. While the children in the scene were playing at the water's edge, 1906, the town mill was grinding grain into meal for pigs and chickens. It is now a car museum. Another attraction is Birdland, developed in the grounds of a former Tudor mansion, where all kinds of exotic birds are to be seen. Bourton church is Georgian, with some interesting additions made between 1875 and 1895. Not far away is Salmonsbury, an Iron Age hill-fort. It was excavated in 1930, and revealed the foundations of circular huts, of wattle and daub, and thatched conical roofs.

58. The 'Old New Inn' at Bourton was built in the eighteenth century, and has a sundial inscribed, Silas Wells 1718. Inside are murals depicting events in Saxon and Roman times. The well-turned-out waggonette, 1906, carried guests to and from the railway station, and made short excursions round the town and into the countryside round about. In the 1930s the vegetable garden behind the inn became the site for a model village − of Bourton itself. The idea was that of the then owner. Some 200 tons of Cotswold stone were carted from a local quarry and, with the help of local masons and craftsmen, the idea was turned into a reality. The houses and roads of the town were measured, the positions of trees and lamp-posts noted, and all were reduced to scale. Water for the miniature Windrush river was pumped from the garden well. The model is one of the great attractions of Bourton.

59. As is evident, Stow-on-the-Wold was a quiet town in 1909. Its hey-day had been in the middle ages, when great fairs for the sale of sheep, wool, and cloth were held. Later horses, cattle, and cheeses were sold as well as sheep. In 1477, Edward IV authorised two fairs, to be held on 24 October and 12 May (new calendar dates). The Market Square is irregular, and enclosed by old houses, inns, and shops, in a variety of styles. The fourteenth century Cross on the right was restored in 1878 when the lantern head, with sculptured figures, was added. At other points about the Square are drinking troughs (1895), and footstocks used in Tudor times. The tower of the church is 80 feet high, and the building can boast of every kind of architecture from Norman to Tudor. In the town museum are exhibits of the Civil War battle fought close by in 1646. The town is now a tourist centre, and prominent in the antique trade.

THE HORSE FAIR, STOW-ON-THE-WOLD

60. The Horse Fair at Stow, here seen in 1912, was also the occasion for manufacturers of horse-drawn farm implements to exhibit them. Anything up to three hundred horses were for sale, made up of hunters, hacks, Welsh ponies, cobs, carthorses, colts and geldings. The fair was a red-letter day for villagers for miles around, and they flocked to it. The horses were well-turned out, particularly the heavy carthorses. Their manes and tails were braided and plaited in red, white and blue ribbons, their coats were given a good sheen, and their hooves were blacked. The carters and grooms who attended them were likewise well-groomed, with clean clothes, fresh neckerchiefs, and polished boots. Other decorative features on the harness of carthorses were horse-brasses, very popular between 1857 and 1900, and exhibited by harness-makers. These brasses are collected today as antiques. The Horse Fair takes place on 12 May.

the quarry Bourton-on-the-Hill

61. Round about 1900 large numbers of quarries were being worked in the Cotswolds, producing stone for building, slating, dry-walling, and road-making. Today there are fewer, but they are vaster and more mechanised. The quality of limestone varied from quarry to quarry. The tighter-grained stone was used for building because it weathered well. It was cut out in large blocks about 2½ feet square, and sawn into shape by hand with a large, steel cross-cut saw. The scene above is typical of a quarry in 1906, showing a swivel-hoist for raising the stone on to the waggon, and a team of heavy horses to pull it out of the quarry to the place where it had to be dressed. The men accompanying the waggon and horses worked a nine-hour day or sixty-hour week on piece work. The stone was measured and they were paid accordingly, getting on average some thirty shillings a week.

62. Chipping Norton Market Place, seen here on a summer's day in 1907, was in existence as far back as 1205. The prefix 'Chipping' was added to Norton in 1224. Great heards of cattle and flocks of sheep were brought to the market by drovers until the coming of the railways in the 1860s when a station was built at the end of Church Street. In their turn, however, railways lost much movement of beasts to road transport as, in the 1920s, motorised cattle-floats were able to deliver their load into the market itself. At either end of the Market Place are the Town Hall, in the eighteenth century Classical style, and the Old Guildhall. In Victorian and Edwardian times, when the Annual Fair took place here at Michaelmas, agricultural workers and maidservants used to stand beside the Town Hall to hire themselves for new jobs during the coming year. The Market Place was a favourite meeting place for the Heythrop Hunt.

CHIPPING NORTON.   CHURCH STREET.

63. Church Street, Chipping Norton, with children resting in the shade beside the typical Cotswold dry-stone wall, seems to be a haven of peace. The date is 1908, and apart from the trim houses on the left, a picturesque group of almshouses stands just above the church which is on a slope below the main street. Built in the Perpendicular style, the church is regarded as one of the finest in Oxfordshire. Its interior is exceptionally light, and in one of its aisles a number of fifteenth and sixteenth century brasses are preserved. The tower in view here was built in 1823 to replace the former one which had become insecure. As with many other Cotswold churches, it owes its existence to a fifteenth-century wool merchant. In this case he was John Ashfield. An unusual story connected with it is that in 1549 its vicar was hanged from the tower by his churchwardens.

64. Chipping Norton was involved in cloth manufacture long before the eighteenth century. In 1821 the firm of Bliss and Sons which, since 1746 had made kersey and horsecloths, now turned to making tweeds. By 1851 they were employing 150 workers, and in 1867 won a gold medallion at the Amsterdam Exhibition. Between 1850 and 1860 the firm appealed for a branch railway line in order to transport their tweeds more quickly. Consequently, the Great Western Railway was built, and so helped to maintain the town's prosperity in the cloth trade for another century. There was a disastrous fire at the mill in 1872, and it was rebuilt in the form shown here, to look like a country house, and to form a notable landmark with its tall tower. A stairway runs through the dome whose parapet is 64 feet from the ground. The chimney is 165 feet high. Bliss Mill was the first to use electricity for light and power. It closed in 1980.

MORETON-IN-MARSH.

65. The two youths are standing in the main street of Moreton-in-Marsh which forms part of the Roman Fosse Way. The eighteenth century Redesdale Arms Hotel on the left was called the Unicorn prior to 1891, and the postcard is dated 1912. Redesdale Market Hall stands on an island site on round pillars, and breaks up the ruler-straight street. It is Victorian, built in the Tudor style with mullioned windows and transomed Tudor-arched heads, in 1887. The arcade has since been enclosed and is used as a store. The steep-pitched roof is of Cotswold slate, and its clock turret stands clear for all to see. Lord Redesdale restored the building and the hotel repeats the name. The town has many other interesting buildings, not least the Mann Institute, built in 1891 to function as a club and meeting house. To the right of the Hall, just off the picture, is a curfew tower, a quaint survival of another age.

LOWER ODDINGTON.   B.3.L.

66. Oddington, comprised of two parts, Upper and Lower, lies east of Stow, and is here seen as a quiet village in the vale of the Evenlode. The light, four-wheeled van by the farm is typical of those used by delivery men at that time. Posters on the wall to the right kept the villagers informed of events of all kinds. Oddington has two churches, St. Nicholas dating from the thirteenth century, and Ascension built in 1852. The former stands in isolation away from the village. In 1907 it was in a bad state of neglect until the rector undertook its restoration. His successor continued the work, and eventually it came into the care of the Society for the Preservation of Ancient Buildings. In 1913 the windowless north wall was uncovered to reveal a fourteenth century Doom Wall Painting, covering 500 square feet, and said to be the best example in England.

The Manor House, Upper Slaughter

67. One of the most beautiful houses in the Cotswolds is Manor House at Upper Slaughter. As can be seen from this 1929 postcard, it has an Elizabethan front and a Jacobean porch. It underwent sympathetic restoration in the late nineteenth century, and about 1913 had a fourth gable added to it. The village lies behind it, with a little stream running through it, to be crossed by two stone bridges and a fording place. Eight cottages near the churchyard were renovated by Sir Edwin Lutyens, the celebrated architect, in 1906. The village church was also renovated in 1877, and several windows were glazed between 1882 and 1900. The Reverend Francis E. Witts was lord of the manor and rector between 1808 and 1854, and his diary was published in 1978. It gives an insight into Cotswold life during that time. The rectory in which he lived is now the Lords of the Manor Hotel.

68. The Post Office, Lower Slaughter, seen here in 1930, has been moved round the corner on the left to the Mill House. Most of the stone cottages, with their trim gardens, are mainly on the north bank of the stream whose banks were lined with stone in the 1900s. In 1890 the waters carried a plentiful supply of trout. The footbridges are of weathered stone, and fit in well with the green verges on either bank. Within living memory the pure water supply of the village came from a spring in a nearby hill, and was piped to a drinking fountain, dated 1875, further up the street. Beyond it is the church, rebuilt in 1867, and adjacent to it is the early seventeenth century Manor House, now a hotel. Within the grounds is a stone dovecote, one of the largest in the Cotswolds, but unique in that it has two compartments, two equal gables with mullioned openings, and a small Tudor doorway.

69. The nineteenth century water-mill at Lower Slaughter was working when this postcard was made in 1930. With the mill-pool, it makes a picturesque scene. However, it is in contrast with the mellow, honey-coloured stone of almost all the houses, cottages, and farmsteads in the village, for it is built of brick. The water-wheel is in situ today, but turns only slowly as a feature of interest to visitors. Now partly used as a bakery, post-office and shop, the mill was nevertheless working until as recently as the 1960s. In close proximity are Mill Cottage, Ivy Cottage, Malthouse Cottage, and others with them, while the large old malthouse itself has been converted into a residence. One further pleasing feature of the village is to be seen in the relatively modern council houses which have been built in stone, with the traditional Cotswold slate roofs. Privately-built houses are also in stone.

Morris Dancers at Lower Slaughter, 17-7-20. Butt, Photographer.

2

70. The scene above, 1920, is unusual in that the dancers are of both sexes. Traditionally, the Morris Dance was an energetic English country dance performed by eight men to the accompaniment of a fiddler. At this time, efforts were being made to revive country dances, and anyone interested could take part. In the famous Bampton Morris Dances, the men dress in white, with flowered and ribboned hats, ribbons on their clothes, and brightly coloured bell-pads on their legs. Six men dance at a time, with two standing out until their turn comes. They also have a 'fool' with a pig's bladder on a stick, and a 'sword-bearer' who carries a large cake in a tin impaled on his sword. The Cotswold Morris men use handkerchiefs, sticks, and hand-claps, with six men, and jigs for a single man or pair. Most old established Morris teams perform at Whitsuntide on village greens or market places.

71. Handbell ringing is to be found in many parts of the Cotswolds, and this Lower Slaughter team posing for their photograph in 1919 was well-known throughout the district. The ringing of handbells as entertainment is of ancient origin, and was associated with religious ritual in the old Greek, Egyptian, and Asiatic civilisations. The earliest bells were of beaten copper, but since the Bronze Age they have been cast both in bronze and copper, as well as in brass. Often they were beautifully decorated. Teams of handbell ringers came into being when sets of bells were tuned to a seven-note scale. In England this occurred in the seventeenth century for practicing mathematical permutations of change-ringing with church bells. By the eighteenth century, ringers had branched out into tune playing, and the range of the bells was expanded to a twelve-note scale. Handbell-ringing is often included as part of village concerts and church festivals.

72. Naunton, consisting of grey stone cottages, houses, and farmsteads, with walls, roofs, gables, and dormer windows setting each other off, is scattered along a mile of the lovely wooded valley of the winding river Windrush. From above, as here in 1930, the village looks serene as the sides of the valley rise smoothly up to meet the green and grey-brown wolds. The church is mainly sixteenth century, but was heavily restored in 1899, when the floor levels were altered. Among the many treasures within is the white stone pulpit, dated about 1400, with its panelled, canopied, and richly decorated oak cornice. In the village is a large and ancient dovecote with four gables, and nesting holes for over a thousand birds. The old manor house which once stood nearby has gone, and the village mill, which ground corn for two centuries, was sold in 1930. Later it was converted into a dwelling house.

73. This is Notgrove station as it was in 1910. It was situated 1½ miles from the village at an elevation of 700 feet on the Great Western Railway Banbury and Cheltenham branch line. It was closed in the 1960s after having served a large area of scattered villages, farms and houses, for many decades. It has now been completely obliterated as a station, and filled in. Only the approach road and a few houses are left. In a field within a few yards of the approach road is a long-barrow, 160 feet long and 80 feet wide, under the care of the Ministry of Works. Admission is free. The barrow was explored in 1880, but more thorough excavations at a later date revealed the bones of a chieftin and nine women, children, and infants, indicating that these were human sacrifices so that the chieftin would not go unattended in the next world. The finds are in Cheltenham museum.

74. Minster Lovell, off the main Burford to Witney road, is fringe Cotswold, but has plenty of stone buildings to give it the right kind of atmosphere. The ruins of its fifteenth century minster are worth seeing, as is the town itself, with the Windrush winding through it. The above circular dovecote was photographed in the 1920s, and stands in the farmyard just north-east of the church. It is typical of many hundreds that were once common in the Cotswolds. They were solidly built, and their inner walls may have had holes for 1,500 birds. Many of them had a ladder inside which rotated round a central wooden pillar, thus bringing every hole within arms reach of a man on the ladder. Dovecotes were owned by the lord of the manor in mediaeval times. Flying birds, which fed on the peasants' corn, were culled and eaten, and a proportion of the squabs in the holes were also taken. Up to 3,000 birds might be eaten in a year.

75. This is a typical harvest scene in the Cotswolds in the mid-1920s. Two strong carthorses and a trace-horse were needed to pull the reaping machine, known as a binder, up the slope of the field. The machine cut and tied the corn into sheaves of a regular weight and size, and the three-pronged arm was automatically set in motion when the sheaf was fully packed. It ejected it on to the stubble. Gangs of workers then had to work along the field, propping the sheaves into upright 'shocks' so that sun and wind could dry them. In due course they were loaded on to waggons and taken to the farm's stackyard. When complete, the stacks were thatched with long wheat straw. Threshing the stacks was done according to the state of the corn-market, often during the winter. The binder was superseded by the combine-harvester after the last war, and the straw is now either baled or burnt on the stubble.

In the North Quadrangle. Sudeley Castle

76. Compared with some parts of the country, the Cotswold region has few castles. One, however, is Sudeley Castle, just south of Winchcombe, enclosed in the gentle folds of the Cotswold scarp. Its military position as chief fortress between Berkeley and Warwick was once important, for it guarded the roads in every direction across the hills between Chipping Campden and Cirencester, and those running westwards to Gloucester and Hereford. Its long history has been connected with kings and queens and statesmen, of England. In the Civil Wars it changed hands several times. Its present appearance owes much to the restorations which took place in Victorian times and from 1930 onwards when the photograph was taken. The castle has days when it is open to the public, and on occasions puts on exhibitions of film and theatrical costumes. Its grounds and buildings have also been the backcloth for film making.